MIND

OVER

MATTER

How to Harness Your Thoughts to Conquer Alcohol and Create a Life You Love

DARYL TYLER

DISCLAIMER NOTICE:

The information presented in this book is provided for informational purposes only and should not be construed as medical or professional advice. The author, publisher, and distributors of this book make no representations or warranties regarding the accuracy, reliability, or completeness of the information contained herein.

The reader should consult a licensed professional before making any decisions related to alcohol use, addiction, or recovery. The author, publisher, and distributors of this book are not responsible for any actions or decisions made by the reader based on the information presented in this book.

The views and opinions expressed in this book are those of the author and do not necessarily reflect the official policy or position of any organization the author may be affiliated with.

The information presented in this book is based on research and experience at the time of publication, and the author, publisher, and distributors of this book cannot guarantee that the information will remain accurate or relevant in the future.

The author, publisher, and distributors of this book disclaim all liability for any loss, damage, or injury caused, or alleged to be caused, directly or indirectly by the information presented in this book.

TABLE OF CONTENTS

Title Page

INTRODUCTION

CHAPTER ONE

THE SCIENCE BEHIND ALCOHOL: INGREDIENTS, CHEMICALS, AND MANUFACTURE

CHAPTER TWO

ALCOHOL CRAVINGS: WHAT ARE THE CAUSES OF ALCOHOL CRAVINGS?
CREATING A PERSONALIZED RECOVERY TOOLKIT: BUILDING YOUR OWN PATH TO SOBRIETY

CHAPTER THREE

EXPLORING THE RELATIONSHIP BETWEEN ALCOHOL AND BRAIN FUNCTION: SHORT AND LONG-TERM EFFECTS
HOW DOES ALCOHOL USE AFFECT BRAIN NEUROPSYCHOLOGY?
DOES ALCOHOL ACTUALLY KILL BRAIN CELLS?

CHAPTER FOUR

ALCOHOL AND ANXIETY
WHY DRINKING TO CALM YOUR NERVES MAY DO MORE HARM THAN GOOD.
ALCOHOL AS A STRESS RELIEVER: SEPARATING FACT FROM FICTION
ALCOHOL HANGOVERS AND ANXIETY: HOW THEY'RE CONNECTED
ALCOHOL AND ANXIETY: WHY MODERATE DRINKING ISN'T
TRADITIONAL WAYS OF TREATING ANXIETY: MEDICATIONS AND THERAPY

LIFESTYLE CHANGES FOR A CALMER YOU: REDUCING ANXIETY WITH DAILY HABITS
COPING WITH ANXIETY: TECHNIQUES TO EASE YOUR MIND

CHAPTER FIVE

LOWERING YOUR CHOLESTEROL: CAN CUT DOWN ON ALCOHOL HELP?
HOW MUCH ALCOHOL IS SAFE TO DRINK?
CAN DRINKING ALCOHOL BENEFIT, HEART HEALTH?
FOCUS ON A HEALTHY LIFESTYLE INSTEAD

CHAPTER SIX

ALCOHOL AND BLOOD PRESSURE: UNDERSTANDING THE CONNECTION
DOES ALCOHOL RAISE OR LOWER BLOOD PRESSURE?
DANGERS OF MIXING ALCOHOL AND BLOOD PRESSURE MEDICATIONS
WILL QUITTING ALCOHOL LOWER BLOOD PRESSURE?
RELATIONSHIP BETWEEN ALCOHOL WITHDRAWAL AND BLOOD PRESSURE

CHAPTER SEVEN

DRINKING WITH DIABETES: WHAT YOU NEED TO KNOW FOR SAFE HAPPY HOUR

CHAPTER EIGHT

THE INTERSECTION OF BIRTH CONTROL AND ALCOHOL: WHAT YOU NEED TO KNOW
IS IT SAFE TO DRINK ALCOHOL ON BIRTH CONTROL?
TYPES OF BIRTH CONTROL AND ALCOHOL'S INFLUENCE ON EFFECTIVENESS

CHAPTER NINE

IS ALCOHOL A CONTROLLED SUBSTANCE?

CONSUMPTION GUIDELINES FOR ALCOHOL: HOW MUCH IS TOO MUCH?

The Immediate and Potential Lasting Effects of Short-Term Alcohol Use
The Long-Term Complications of Excessive Alcohol Use
Regulating Controlled and Uncontrolled Substances:
Understanding the Difference

CHAPTER TEN

The Stages of Alcoholism: Understanding the Progression of Addiction
Signs and Symptoms of Each Stage:

CHAPTER ELEVEN

How to Break Free from Alcohol Addiction without AA: Expert Tips and Strategies

CHAPTER TWELVE

Life After Recovery: Navigating Relationships, Careers, and Finding Purpose

CONCLUSION

INTRODUCTION

I was a heavy drinker for most of my adult life. I didn't think much of it at first, just a way to unwind after work or to socialize with friends. But over time, it became clear that alcohol was becoming more than just a casual indulgence.

I started drinking earlier in the day, hiding bottles around the house so I could sneak a drink whenever I wanted. I'd lie to my loved ones about how much I was drinking, telling them I was cutting back when really, I was drinking more than ever. I was getting into arguments with my spouse and my friends, and my work was suffering too.

I knew I needed to make a change, but every time I tried to quit drinking, I found myself struggling. My mind was constantly fixated on alcohol, and I couldn't shake the cravings no matter how hard I tried. I felt like I was trapped in a vicious cycle, unable to break free from my addiction.

That's when I discovered the power of mind over matter. I began to study techniques to harness my thoughts and control my cravings. I learned to recognize the triggers that led me to drink and to replace those triggers with positive habits.

It wasn't easy, but with each passing day, I felt stronger and more in control. I began to enjoy the small things in life that I had neglected for so long, like spending time with my family and pursuing my hobbies. I found myself feeling happier and more content than I had in years.

Now, I'm proud to say that I've been sober for over a year. Mind over matter has been the key to my success. By focusing on my thoughts and using them to create positive change in my life, I've been able to conquer alcohol and create a life that I truly love.

If you're struggling with addiction, I encourage you to explore the power of your mind. You have the ability to control your thoughts and use them to shape your future. With the right mindset, anything is possible.

According to a study published in the Journal of the American Medical Association, individuals who believe they have a drinking problem are less likely to seek treatment than those who don't believe they have a problem, even if they exhibit the same symptoms and behaviors. This shocking fact underscores the importance of harnessing the power of the mind to overcome addiction, as individuals who believe they can conquer alcohol and create a better life for themselves are more likely to take the necessary steps to make that a reality.

One uncommon belief that is explored in "Mind Over Matter: How to Harness Your Thoughts to Conquer Alcohol and Create a Life You Love" is the idea that our thoughts and beliefs about alcohol are often more important than the physical effects of the substance itself. This belief suggests that by changing our perception of alcohol and its role in our lives, we can overcome addiction and create a more fulfilling life. While it may seem counterintuitive, this approach has been successful for many people and highlights the importance of the mind-body connection in addiction recovery.

"Mind Over Matter is a book for anyone who is struggling with alcohol addiction and is looking for a new approach to recovery. Whether you have tried traditional methods of treatment and have not found success or are just beginning to explore your options, this book offers a fresh perspective on addiction recovery that focuses on the power of the mind. The techniques and insights presented in this book are applicable to anyone who wants to create positive change in their life, regardless of their background or circumstances. With practical advice and real-life examples, this book offers a roadmap for those who are ready to

take control of their thoughts and transform their relationship with alcohol.

While "Mind Over Matter: How to Harness Your Thoughts to Conquer Alcohol and Create a Life You Love" offers a unique and effective approach to addiction recovery, it may not be suitable for everyone. This book is not for those who are not willing to put in the effort to make significant changes in their lives. It is also not for those who are looking for a quick fix or a one-size-fits-all solution to addiction. This book requires a willingness to examine and challenge one's beliefs and thought patterns, which can be a difficult and uncomfortable process. Additionally, those who have severe physical or mental health issues related to alcohol addiction may require additional support beyond what is offered in this book. While "Mind Over Matter" can be a valuable resource for many, it may not be the right fit for everyone.

- ❖ Are you tired of feeling trapped in a cycle of alcohol addiction, where every day feels like a struggle just to get through?

- ❖ Do you want more out of life than just going through the motions, feeling like you're missing out on the joys and opportunities that sobriety can offer?

- ❖ Are you ready for a new approach to addiction recovery that focuses on the power of your own mind and beliefs, empowering you to take control of your life and create a fulfilling, alcohol-free future?

- ✓ If you answered yes to any of these questions, then "Mind Over Matter: How to Harness Your Thoughts to Conquer Alcohol and Create a Life You Love" may be just what you need. This book offers a unique and effective approach to addiction recovery that focuses on changing your mindset and harnessing the power of your thoughts to conquer alcohol addiction and create a life that you truly love.

Through "Mind Over Matter," you can learn practical techniques and strategies for shifting your mindset, breaking free from the grip of addiction, and creating a life that you truly love. Whether you've tried other methods of treatment and haven't found success, or you're just beginning to explore your options, this book provides a roadmap for transforming your relationship with alcohol and unlocking your full potential.

By tapping into the power of your own thoughts and beliefs, you can overcome addiction, reduce stress and anxiety, improve your relationships, and create a life that is filled with joy, purpose, and meaning. With "Mind Over Matter," the possibilities are endless. So why wait? Take the first step towards a brighter, alcohol-free future by diving into "Mind Over Matter" now!

CHAPTER ONE

THE SCIENCE BEHIND ALCOHOL: INGREDIENTS, CHEMICALS, AND MANUFACTURE

Alcohol is a popular beverage consumed worldwide, but do you know what it is and how it affects your body? Let's take a closer look at the science behind alcohol.

In scientific terms, alcohol is a group of molecules formed when oxygen and hydrogen atoms bind with an atom of carbon. However, when it comes to alcoholic drinks, the alcohol we consume is specifically ethanol. Ethanol is a small molecule that affects the body every time you drink it.

When you drink alcohol, ethanol molecules are absorbed into your bloodstream and travel to virtually all parts of your body, including your brain. Alcohol suppresses normal activity around the brain that controls inhibition, leading to a depressant effect. As the alcohol wears off, your brain must readjust, which can contribute to feelings of anxiety.

While alcohol may be enjoyed by many, it's important to recognize that it's also toxic to the body. As a result, your body must work to get rid of it every time you drink. Consuming several alcoholic drinks in a short space of time puts you at risk of acute alcohol poisoning. Additionally, drinking heavily for months or years increases your risk of developing several types of cancer and other serious health problems.

IS ALCOHOL A DRUG?

Alcohol is recognized as a psychoactive substance by the World Health Organization, which places it in the same category as other drugs, including many illegal ones. However, alcohol isn't legally classified as a drug in the UK. Even so, laws are in place to control its sale, such as making it illegal for under-18s to buy alcohol.

HOW IS ALCOHOL MADE?

Alcohol is made by fermenting grains, fruits, or vegetables. Fermentation is a chemical reaction where yeast or bacteria react with the sugars in the other ingredients to produce ethanol and carbon dioxide. One unit of alcohol is 10ml or 8g of pure alcohol, and it takes an average adult around an hour to process one unit.

Wine and cider are made by fermenting fruit, while fermented cereals like barley and rye form the basis of beer and spirits. Spirits go through a process called distillation, where a proportion of the water is removed, leaving a stronger concentration of alcohol in the final product. The alcohol content of a drink is affected by how long it's left to ferment.

Finally, Alcohol is a widely consumed beverage, but it's essential to understand its chemical makeup and how it affects the body. By being aware of these facts, you can make informed decisions about your alcohol consumption and its potential impact on your health.

CHAPTER TWO

ALCOHOL CRAVINGS: WHAT ARE THE CAUSES OF ALCOHOL CRAVINGS?

There are various explanations suggested by experts regarding the causes of cravings.

> **ALTERATIONS IN THE CHEMICAL COMPOSITION OF THE BRAIN.**

Alcohol consumption can lead to changes in brain chemistry, which can contribute to the development of cravings. Regular heavy drinking can alter the levels of certain neurotransmitters in the brain, such as dopamine and GABA, which are responsible for regulating pleasure and anxiety, respectively. As a result, the brain can become more dependent on alcohol to produce these feelings, leading to an increased desire to drink. Over time, these changes can become more entrenched, making it harder to quit drinking and leading to more intense cravings.

➢ THE PROCESS OF FORMING A HABIT

Alcohol can impact your brain in various ways, and one of them is the formation of habits. Many people begin to use alcohol on a regular basis because they experience positive feelings or an improved mood after drinking. For instance, having a drink after an unpleasant argument with a partner can help one feel calmer, or having a drink after a challenging day at work can help with relaxation.

Additionally, alcohol consumption at social events can help with socializing. The positive feelings that occur when drinking creates a sense of reward, which reinforces the desire to drink in certain situations. Eventually, this reward-seeking behavior can lead to cravings for alcohol in new situations.

➢ TRIGGERS

Cravings frequently occur as an unconscious reaction to a trigger, which can be a recollection of something related to alcohol or an emotion like stress. Typically, individuals who encounter cravings observe a combination of both internal and external triggers.

When it comes to experiencing cravings, both internal and external triggers can play a role. Internal triggers are those that originate from within, such as memories, thoughts, emotions, or physical sensations that can provoke the desire to drink. Feeling sad, anxious, stressed, angry, or physically uncomfortable can all serve as internal triggers.

On the other hand, external triggers involve environmental cues that you associate with drinking. These may include specific places, times, people, or situations. For example, going to a restaurant or bar where you usually drink, attending a party, finishing work for the day, or having an argument with a parent can all trigger the desire to drink.

Being aware of both your internal and external triggers can be helpful in managing your cravings and reducing the likelihood of relapse. By recognizing what prompts your desire to drink, you can take steps to avoid or cope with those triggers in a more constructive way.

In the heat of a craving, it can be tempting to give in and reach for a drink. But there are ways to cope with the intensity of the moment. One effective approach is simply to recognize the craving for what it is and ride it out. Keep in mind that the urge to drink typically only lasts a few minutes before subsiding.

To help get through those few minutes, there are several things you can try. For example, you might distract yourself by engaging in a favorite activity or hobby. Going for a walk, listening to music, or practicing deep breathing can also help take your mind off the craving.

Another helpful tactic is to replace the drink with a non-alcoholic alternative that you enjoy. This could be a favorite beverage, a healthy snack, or even a piece of candy. The act of consuming something can help satisfy the urge for a drink and give you a sense of control over the situation.

> ➤ Finally, it's important to reach out for support if you're struggling with cravings. Whether it's a trusted friend, family member, or professional counselor, having someone to talk to can help you stay focused on your goals and avoid giving in to the temptation to drink.

> ➤ **DISTRACTING YOURSELF IN POSITIVE WAYS**

When a craving for alcohol hits, it can be challenging to focus on anything else. However, distracting yourself with a positive activity can be a helpful technique to ease the urge to drink. One way to be prepared is to create a list of potential distractions and keep it in a convenient location, such as on your phone, fridge, or in a journal.

Here are a few activities to consider:

- Crank up some music and dance.
- Escape into a good book for a chapter.
- Take a stroll, either by yourself or with a friend or pet.
- Watch a funny TV show or movie.
- Make a snack or brew a cup of tea.
- Tackle a decluttering project, like organizing a drawer.
- Practice some mindful coloring.
- Spend some time on your favorite hobby.

Other strategies that may help include meditation, reaching out to a sober friend, or taking a refreshing shower.

> ➢ **REACHING OUT TO FRIENDS AND FAMILY**

Connecting with a supportive friend or family member can be a powerful tool for managing cravings. Whether they're also trying to quit drinking or simply there to listen, having someone to turn to can provide a much-needed sense of connection and understanding. Even a brief conversation can help shift your focus away from the craving and onto the present moment. Try calling a loved one to chat, meeting up for a walk, or sharing a meal together. Remember, human connection is a powerful antidote to the isolation that can come with addiction, and reaching out to others can help you stay on track with your goals.

> ➤ **MINDFULNESS TECHNIQUES TO COMBAT CRAVINGS**

Staying present is a powerful tool when it comes to dealing with cravings. Mindfulness exercises can help you focus your mind and calm your emotions. By anchoring your awareness in the present moment, you can soothe yourself until the craving subsides.

Here are a few techniques to try:

- **Deep breathing or relaxation exercises:** Take a few deep breaths and focus your attention on your breath. You can also try progressive muscle relaxation, where you tense and then relax different muscle groups throughout your body.

- **Grounding techniques:** Use your senses to anchor yourself in the present moment. For example, you might focus on the sensation of your feet on the ground, the texture of your clothes, or the sounds around you.

- **Physical activity, including yoga or stretches**: Exercise can help release tension and reduce stress. Yoga and stretching can also help you connect with your body and release pent-up emotions.

- **Changing your environment**: Sometimes a change of scenery can help shift your mood and distract you from your cravings. Take a walk, go outside, or move to a different room in your home.

➢ **APPROACH CRAVINGS WITH CURIOSITY**

When facing a craving, it's common to feel a sense of restriction or resistance. However, approaching the craving with curiosity can be a helpful technique to manage the urge to drink. Instead of trying to suppress the craving, try acknowledging it and examining it with an open mind.

Here are a few ways to embrace curiosity when facing a craving:

- Ask yourself how it would feel to move through the craving without drinking.
- Address your brain directly and acknowledge the craving, saying something like, "I hear you want a drink, but let's try something new and see how it feels."

By approaching your cravings with curiosity, you can better understand your triggers and learn more about your relationship with alcohol. This can help you make more informed decisions about how to respond to cravings in the future.

Transforming your relationship with alcohol is a journey that requires commitment and long-term strategies.

Here are a few ideas to consider:

- **Build a support network**: Create a network of friends, family, or professionals who understand your goals and can offer guidance when needed. Consider attending a support group or therapy to get extra support and accountability.
- **Develop healthy habits:** Building healthy habits such as regular exercise, good sleep hygiene, and a nutritious diet can not only improve your physical health but also help you cope with stress and manage cravings.
- **Identify and address underlying issues:** If you find that alcohol has become a way to cope

with underlying issues like anxiety or depression, it's important to address these issues with the help of a professional.

- **Practice self-compassion**: Be gentle with yourself as you work towards your goals. Recognize that setbacks and slip-ups are a natural part of the process and use them as an opportunity to learn and grow.
- **Reframe your mindset**: Shift your focus from what you are giving up to what you are gaining. Think about the benefits of sobriety, such as improved health, better relationships, and increased productivity.

➢ **TAKE CONTROL OF YOUR TRIGGERS**

Understanding what triggers your urge to drink a crucial step toward long-term recovery is. By identifying specific people, places, and situations that cue your cravings, you can take control of your triggers and avoid them as much as possible. This is especially important in the early stages of recovery, as triggers are often most intense when you first stop drinking.

Some ways to avoid your triggers might include moving your wine rack out of sight or giving it away, choosing alcohol-free restaurants, hanging out with friends at times that don't involve drinking or changing up your commute to avoid passing your favorite bar.

Practicing good self-care, such as getting enough sleep, eating well, staying hydrated, and spending time with supportive companions, can also help address underlying needs that may fuel your cravings.

However, avoiding triggers alone may not be enough to make lasting changes. You may also need to learn to work through difficult emotions and handle challenging situations in more productive ways. For example, if you experience your strongest cravings when you're feeling anxious or stressed or facing conflict with someone you care about, developing healthy coping mechanisms can help you better manage these situations and reduce the urge to drink.

Creating a Personalized Recovery Toolkit: Building Your Own Path to Sobriety

The road to recovery is not a one-size-fits-all journey. Each person has their own unique challenges and triggers when it comes to managing alcohol cravings. That's why it's crucial to create a personalized toolkit that works for you and helps you navigate the ups and downs of sobriety.

- **Build a Physical and Invisible Toolkit**
  Your toolkit can take many forms, from an actual physical box filled with comforting items like your favorite book, a soothing tea, or a sentimental object, to an "invisible" toolkit consisting of mindfulness exercises, positive affirmations, and breathing techniques.

- **Take Control of Your Recovery**

  As you build your toolkit, remember that you are the architect of your own recovery. Think of it as a creative act, where you are painting your own journey with every stroke. By taking control of your recovery, you are building a safety net around yourself that will help you stay on track during the most challenging times.

- **Customize Your Toolkit**

  Since each person's journey is unique, what works for someone else might not work for you. That's why it's essential to experiment with different strategies and find what helps you the most. Maybe it's a yoga class, an inspiring podcast, or a support group that resonates with you. Whatever it is, keep it in your toolkit and use it when you need it.

In summary, building a personalized recovery toolkit is a vital step toward long-term sobriety. By creating your own path, you can navigate your journey with confidence and strength, knowing that you have the tools you need to overcome any obstacle that comes your way.

CHAPTER THREE

Exploring the Relationship Between Alcohol and Brain Function: Short and Long-Term Effects

Alcohol is known to impact the brain in various ways, causing functional impairments and behavioral changes that can be long-lasting. The brain is responsible for regulating virtually every process in our bodies, including memory, emotion, and motor skills, making it critical to understand the impact of alcohol use on the brain. This article will delve into the short-term and long-term effects of alcohol on the brain, including how it affects memory, executive functions, visuospatial abilities, mental health, and psychomotor abilities.

How Does Alcohol Use Affect Brain Neuropsychology?

Alcohol can impair several critical brain functions, leading to both short-term and long-term consequences. Short-term memory loss is one of the earliest impacts of alcohol on the brain. Memory is classified as short-term and long-term, and as a person's blood alcohol content increases, memory impairment also increases. Drinking alcohol can hinder the recollection of short-term memories and potentially lead to their complete elimination, causing a blackout. The hippocampus, which is accountable for memory consolidation, is especially vulnerable during a blackout, and an individual may have little or no recollection of the events that took place under the influence of alcohol. Long-term memory loss can also occur due to extended alcohol use, leading to alcohol-related dementia.

Alcohol use can also impair executive functions, known as the "management system" of the brain. Alcohol suppresses activity in the prefrontal cortex, leading to judgment, problem-solving, decision-making, attention span, perception, and language impairments. Excessive alcohol use over time can damage brain cells within the prefrontal cortex, leading to long-term symptoms such as problems with processing new information, gaining new skills, and formulating plans.

Visuospatial abilities are also impaired by alcohol, which is responsible for how we understand what we see around us. Alcohol's depressant effect slows and impairs visuospatial abilities, leading to difficulties locating objects, reading, and recognizing depth perception. Long-term alcohol use can lead to further impairments, such as a decrease in peripheral vision and, in rare cases, vision loss.

The use of alcohol also has an impact on mental health. Alcohol impacts the striatum, which produces feelings of reward and pleasure, and the amygdala, responsible for emotions. This can create an unhealthy cycle of relying on alcohol to experience joy or elation. While alcohol can provide short-term relief, it ultimately leads to increased discomfort, disrupts, and depletes hormones that impact our mood and exacerbates feelings of depression and anxiety.

Finally, alcohol can impair psychomotor abilities, which connect the brain and muscles. Alcohol's impact on the parietal lobe and the cerebellum creates a disconnect between the brain and body, resulting in impaired coordination, slowed reaction times, difficulties with balance, and poor hand-eye coordination. Over time, unhealthy alcohol use can create more permanent impairments in these brain areas, resulting in psychomotor consequences even when someone is not intoxicated.

Does Alcohol Actually Kill Brain Cells?

Contrary to popular belief, alcohol consumption does not lead to the death of brain cells or neurons. Instead, it leads to a breakdown in cell communication, making it harder for brain cells to fire electrical messages that are essential for normal brain communication and function.

In conclusion, alcohol can have significant effects on brain function and behavior, impacting memory, executive function, visuospatial abilities, mental health, and psychomotor abilities. While some of these effects may be temporary and reversible, others can have long-lasting consequences that persist even after someone stops drinking. Understanding how alcohol affects the brain can help individuals make informed decisions about their alcohol use and take steps to reduce or eliminate their consumption to protect their brain health and well-being. It's important to prioritize healthy habits and seek support when needed, to maintain a healthy and balanced life.

CHAPTER FOUR

Alcohol and Anxiety

Why drinking to calm your nerves may do more harm than good.

It's common to turn to alcohol when feeling anxious or stressed, but relying on it to calm your nerves can have the opposite effect. Studies show that heavy and prolonged alcohol use can increase anxiety levels and even trigger anxiety disorders.

If you're being treated for anxiety, it's important to avoid alcohol altogether or at least limit your intake to moderate levels. Alcohol can interfere with the effectiveness of anxiety medications and worsen their side effects.

Instead of reaching for a drink, consider other healthy ways to cope with stress and anxiety, such as exercise, meditation, or therapy. By addressing the root cause of your anxiety and finding healthy ways to manage it, you can reduce the need for alcohol and improve your overall well-being.

Alcohol as a Stress Reliever: Separating Fact from Fiction

It's no secret that many people turn to alcohol to unwind and alleviate stress. After all, alcohol is a sedative and a depressant that can have a calming effect on the body and mind. However, while it may offer temporary relief, drinking excessively over the long term can increase anxiety and worsen mental health issues.

While the occasional drink under the guidance of a medical professional may be harmless, relying on alcohol as a crutch to cope with stress and anxiety can lead to tolerance, diminishing the positive effects of alcohol on the mind and body. Moreover, excessive alcohol consumption can result in memory loss, blackouts, and other negative physical and mental consequences, which can further exacerbate feelings of anxiety.

It's essential to recognize that alcohol is not a healthy or sustainable coping mechanism for managing stress and anxiety. Instead, individuals should focus on developing healthy habits, such as regular exercise, mindfulness practices, and seeking professional help, if necessary, to promote long-term physical and mental well-being.

The science behind the relaxing effects of alcohol is linked to its impact on blood alcohol content (BAC). Initially, when BAC levels rise, individuals may experience a temporary sense of excitement and euphoria. However, as BAC levels drop, feelings of depression and anxiety can occur. Therefore, it's plausible that consuming a few drinks that cause your BAC levels to rise and fall can leave you feeling even more anxious than before.

The dangers of self-medication

Using alcohol to self-medicate anxiety can be a dangerous cycle. While drinking may initially provide temporary relief, it can lead to a worsening of anxiety symptoms in the long term. In addition, excessive alcohol consumption can lead to dependence, making it more difficult to cope with anxiety without alcohol.

If you're struggling with anxiety, it's important to seek professional help. Your doctor can help you develop a treatment plan that may include therapy, medication, and lifestyle changes. With proper treatment, you can learn healthy coping mechanisms and live a fulfilling life without relying on alcohol to manage your anxiety.

Alcohol Hangovers and Anxiety: How They're Connected

After a night of heavy drinking, you may find yourself feeling more anxious than you were before you started. This is because overconsumption of alcohol can lead to hangovers, which cause symptoms like headaches, dizziness, nausea, dehydration, and low blood sugar that exacerbate anxiety.

Alcohol abuse can also have long-term consequences on mental health, with heavy drinkers being more predisposed to developing an anxiety disorder. In fact, research shows that people with alcoholism have a harder time recovering from traumatic events due to the changes in brain activity caused by alcohol abuse.

While there is no evidence that moderate drinking will cause anxiety, suddenly stopping heavy alcohol consumption can lead to alcohol withdrawal symptoms, including increased anxiety, trembling hands, sweating, a rapid heart rate, hallucinations, nausea, vomiting, and even seizures.

It's essential to recognize the potential negative effects of alcohol on mental health, especially if you suffer from anxiety or other mental health disorders. If you find yourself relying on alcohol to cope with anxiety or social situations, seek professional help to find healthier coping mechanisms.

Alcohol and Anxiety: Why Moderate Drinking Isn't Always Safe

Alcohol consumption is often viewed as a way to unwind and alleviate stress. However, the relationship between alcohol and anxiety is more complex than many people realize. While moderate drinking may be safe for some, it's not a one-size-fits-all solution.

Moderate drinking is generally defined as no more than two drinks per day for adult men and one for women. But age and gender aren't the only factors that determine how much alcohol is safe for you. If you have a low tolerance for drinking, anxious or aggressive tendencies, or a mental health disorder, even moderate drinking may not be safe for you.

Moreover, the benefits of alcohol consumption are often outweighed by the risks, which include depression, obesity, liver disease, and cardiovascular damage. Alcohol also affects everyone differently, and the benefits you might experience from moderate drinking can quickly be undermined by the risks.

If you have anxiety, it's important to seek help from a mental health professional rather than relying on alcohol as a treatment. While alcohol may temporarily alleviate anxiety, it can also worsen it in the long term. And if you think you have a problem with alcohol, seek help from your doctor immediately. Remember, alcohol is not a safe or effective treatment for anxiety, and seeking professional help is the best way to manage anxiety and related issues.

Traditional Ways of Treating Anxiety: Medications and Therapy

Anxiety disorders can be effectively treated with medication and therapy. Depending on the type of anxiety you have, your doctor may recommend different treatment options.

Medications can include antidepressants, which are taken daily to help manage anxiety symptoms, or benzodiazepines, which provide temporary relief from uncontrollable feelings of anxiety. It's important to talk to your doctor about any medications you are taking, as they may interact with alcohol.

Therapy can also be an effective way to manage anxiety. Cognitive behavioral therapy (CBT) can help you learn skills and behaviors to stop avoiding activities due to anxiety, while therapy can also help you explore the root causes of your anxiety and develop coping strategies.

If you have social anxiety, your doctor may recommend therapy combined with medication, such as sertraline, to reduce your anxiety levels. It's important to work with your doctor to find the best treatment plan for you.

Remember, alcohol is not a treatment for anxiety. If you're struggling with anxiety, seek help from a mental health professional or talk to your doctor about treatment options.

Lifestyle Changes for a Calmer You: Reducing Anxiety with

Daily Habits

While anxiety may not always be curable, there are daily lifestyle changes you can make to help reduce its impact and learn how to manage it.

Here are some practical steps you can take to reduce your anxiety on a daily basis:

- **Get Sufficient Sleep:** Aim for 6 to 8 hours of quality sleep each night, depending on your age. Creating a consistent sleep schedule can also help improve your sleep quality.

- **Limit Caffeine and Alcohol:** Consuming too much caffeine or alcohol can increase your anxiety levels. Try to limit your intake of both to see if it makes a difference.

- **Eat Healthily:** Consistently eating healthy and balanced meals can help you maintain stable blood sugar levels, which can prevent mood swings and anxiety.

- **Relaxation Techniques**: Spend some time each day focusing on relaxation techniques like meditation or yoga. This can help to calm your mind and reduce feelings of anxiety.

- **Engage in Relaxing Hobbies**: Set aside time for activities that help you relax and enjoy yourself, such as listening to music, reading a book, or painting. These can help to distract your mind from anxious thoughts and improve your overall mood.

By incorporating these lifestyle changes into your daily routine, you can start to take control of your anxiety and improve your overall well-being. If you are struggling with anxiety, consider speaking with a mental health professional for additional support and guidance.

Coping with Anxiety: Techniques to Ease Your Mind

Dealing with anxiety can be a challenging experience, but there are practical techniques that you can utilize to help you manage it. If you feel overwhelmed by your anxiety, try these methods to slow it down and prevent it from escalating into a panic attack:

- **Practice Deep Breathing:** Slow, controlled breathing is one of the most effective ways to calm yourself down when you feel anxious. Breathe in deeply through your nose and exhale slowly through your mouth, concentrating on the sensation of your breath. This technique can help regulate your heart rate and reduce feelings of tension.

- **Focus on Positive Thoughts:** When you feel negative or anxious thoughts creeping in, try to replace them with more positive ones. Think about something that makes you feel happy or accomplished or try visualizing a peaceful scene.

- **Count to Calm:** Another helpful technique is counting slowly to distract yourself from your anxiety. Start counting from 1 to 10, and if you need more time, continue counting higher.

This can help take your mind off your anxiety and bring you back to the present moment.

- **Engage in Relaxing Activities:** Sometimes, engaging in activities that make you feel good can be an excellent way to cope with anxiety. Listen to some calming music or take up a relaxing hobby, like painting or gardening. Focusing on something that brings you joy can help you forget about your worries and reduce your anxiety levels.

Remember, coping with anxiety is a process, and everyone's experience is different. With time and practice, you can learn to manage your anxiety and take control of your life. If your anxiety is causing significant distress or impairment, seek professional help from a mental health provider.

CHAPTER FIVE

Lowering Your Cholesterol: Can Cut Down on Alcohol Help?

If you're looking to improve your cholesterol levels, cutting back on alcohol may be a good place to start. Not only can it help lower your cholesterol, but it can also have positive effects on your heart, liver, blood pressure, weight, and more.

How Alcohol Affects Cholesterol Levels

When you drink alcohol, your liver breaks it down into triglycerides and cholesterol. This can lead to an increase in your blood levels of both of these substances, which in turn can raise your risk of heart disease. Additionally, alcohol can contribute to the development of fatty liver disease, which can make it harder for your liver to remove cholesterol from your bloodstream.

Other Health Risks of Drinking Alcohol

In addition to raising cholesterol and triglyceride levels, drinking alcohol can also increase your risk of weight gain, high blood pressure, and certain types of cancer. It can also lead to liver disease, pancreatitis, depression, and alcohol dependency.

How Much Alcohol is Safe to Drink?

To stay healthy and avoid illness, the UK government recommends drinking no more than 14 units of alcohol per week for both men and women. It's also important to spread your units out over the week, have some alcohol-free days, and avoid binge drinking.

Can Drinking Alcohol Benefit, Heart Health?

While there was once some belief that drinking alcohol in moderation could be good for your heart, this theory is no longer widely accepted. The only possible benefits are seen in women over the age of 55 who drink 5 or fewer units per week, and even then, the benefits are modest.

Focus on a Healthy Lifestyle Instead

Ultimately, the best way to improve your health is by adopting healthy habits such as eating well and exercising regularly. While cutting back on alcohol may help lower your cholesterol levels, it's important to weigh the risks and benefits and to speak with your doctor if you have any concerns.

CHAPTER SIX

Alcohol and Blood Pressure: Understanding the Connection

High blood pressure affects nearly half of all adults in the United States, and heavy alcohol use can exacerbate the problem. While a drink or two may cause a temporary drop in blood pressure, heavy drinking can lead to chronically elevated blood pressure or hypertension. In this article, we'll explore the effects of alcohol on blood pressure, including the myth of alcohol as a blood pressure regulator, the dangers of mixing alcohol with blood pressure medications, and the relationship between alcohol withdrawal and blood pressure.

How Does Alcohol Affect Blood Pressure?

Blood pressure is the measurement of how hard blood is pushing against the walls of the blood vessels as the heart pumps blood. High blood pressure can cause stress on blood vessels and organs, leading to health problems like kidney disease, heart attack, and stroke.

Heavy alcohol use has two effects on blood pressure. It causes a drop in blood pressure right after drinking and then an increase in blood pressure around 12 hours after drinking. When alcohol is used heavily for a prolonged period, it can lead to chronically elevated blood pressure.

There are many alcohol-related factors that can increase blood pressure, including increased renin, baroreceptor effects, increased cortisol, nervous system changes, and increased calcium levels. These factors can lead to fluid retention, blood vessel constriction, stress hormone increases, sympathetic nervous system changes, and arterial constriction.

Does Alcohol Raise or Lower Blood Pressure?

Contrary to popular belief, alcohol is not a healthy tool for controlling blood pressure and staying healthy. While a small amount of alcohol may cause a brief drop in blood pressure, heavy drinking can lead to long-term high blood pressure and other health issues.

The myth that red wine is good for blood pressure and heart health is inaccurate. The benefits attributed to red wine are likely due to lifestyle factors or the grapes it contains, not the alcohol itself.

Dangers of Mixing Alcohol and Blood Pressure Medications

Alcohol and blood pressure medications should generally not be mixed. Alcohol is difficult for the body to process and adds stress to the liver. This can cause blood pressure medications to stay active in the bloodstream for longer, increasing their effects and potentially causing dangerous drops in blood pressure.

Additionally, alcohol can cause a temporary drop in blood pressure right after drinking. Combined with the effects of blood pressure medication, this can cause dizziness or fainting.

Will Quitting Alcohol Lower Blood Pressure?

Alcohol is a significant contributor to high blood pressure in about 16% of adults in the United States. Quitting alcohol can lead to a significant decrease in blood pressure within days or weeks. However, people struggling to give up drinking should seek help from medical professionals to oversee the withdrawal and recovery process. Alcohol withdrawal can cause dangerous spikes in blood pressure, particularly in heavy drinkers.

Relationship Between Alcohol Withdrawal and Blood Pressure

While becoming sober can help normalize blood pressure in the long term, alcohol withdrawal can cause dangerous spikes in blood pressure. Anyone trying to quit drinking should seek medical help to safely detox from alcohol and manage withdrawal symptoms. Substance use professionals can help people gradually taper off alcohol and monitor their heart rate and blood pressure to prevent dangerous side effects.

Finally, Alcohol and high blood pressure do not mix. While a small amount of alcohol may cause a temporary drop in blood pressure, heavy drinking can lead to chronically elevated blood pressure and other health issues. People who drink heavily or take blood pressure medication should talk to their doctor about the effects of alcohol on their blood pressure. Anyone struggling to give up drinking should seek help from medical professionals to safely detox from alcohol and manage withdrawal symptoms.

CHAPTER SEVEN

Drinking with Diabetes: What You Need to Know for Safe Happy Hour

Living with diabetes can be challenging enough without having to navigate the complicated world of alcohol. If you have diabetes, you may be hesitant to indulge in a cocktail or glass of wine due to concerns about how it will affect your health. However, moderate drinking can have some benefits for people with diabetes, including better blood sugar management and insulin sensitivity. But, as with everything related to diabetes, there are also risks to be aware of.

Here's what you need to know to enjoy a safe happy hour.

The Benefits of Moderate Drinking for Diabetes

Moderate drinking can offer some potential benefits for people with diabetes. Studies have shown that a daily drink or two can improve blood sugar management and insulin sensitivity, which may lead to a lower A1C. However, it's important to note that moderation is key. Drinking more than two drinks per day can lead to higher blood sugar and A1C levels.

So, what is considered moderate drinking? For women, it's one drink per day, and for men, it's up to two drinks per day. But it's important to remember that a "drink" is defined as 5 ounces of wine, a 12-ounce beer, or 1.5 ounces of 80-proof spirits. Drinking larger quantities or more frequently than this can lead to health risks.

The Risks of Drinking Alcohol with Diabetes

While moderate drinking can have benefits, it also comes with risks. The biggest concern for people with diabetes is hypoglycemia or low blood sugar. Drinking alcohol, particularly on an empty stomach, can lead to hypoglycemia when combined with medications used to treat diabetes, such as insulin and sulfonylureas.

Your liver plays a crucial role in stabilizing glucose levels, but it prioritizes metabolizing alcohol over maintaining blood sugar. This can lead to hypoglycemia if you drink without eating food. It can be difficult to distinguish between the symptoms of hypoglycemia and being drunk, especially if you have hypoglycemia unawareness.

Another challenge with drinking alcohol and diabetes is carbohydrate confusion. Alcohol differs from protein, fat, and carbohydrates in that it does not depend on insulin to provide energy to the body. Many people assume that alcoholic drinks are loaded with carbs, but in reality, wine and spirits are practically carbohydrate-free. However, sweet dessert wines do contain a significant amount of carbohydrates.

Drinking alcohol can also lead to calorie confusion and make it easy to lose track of what you're eating. This can lead to weight gain and can even make it easy to mix up medications or forget to take them entirely.

When it comes to drinking and diabetes, there is no one-size-fits-all approach. It's important to talk to your doctor about your drinking habits and get their advice on how to drink in a way that works for you. Remember to drink in moderation, always eat food when drinking, and be mindful of the carb and calorie content of your drinks. With the right precautions and guidance, you can still enjoy a safe and enjoyable happy hour.

CHAPTER EIGHT

The Intersection of Birth Control and Alcohol: What You Need to Know

When it comes to women's health, birth control, and alcohol consumption are two topics that frequently come up in discussions. While most adult women in the United States use some form of birth control and consume alcohol, there may be concerns about the impact of alcohol on the effectiveness of contraception.

This chapter delves into the connection between birth control and alcohol, exploring whether it's safe to drink while using contraceptives and examining potential risks and effects. By providing important information on the topic, I hope to empower women to make informed decisions about their health and well-being.

How Alcohol Affects Birth Control

Before delving into the relationship between birth control and alcohol, it's essential to understand what birth control is and the different forms it takes. **Birth control** refers to any method used to prevent pregnancy, from intrauterine devices (IUDs) and contraceptive injections to pills, patches, condoms, and more.

While alcohol has not been found to reduce or change the efficacy of birth control overall, it's worth noting that it can impair judgment and behavior, which may interfere with the consistent and compliant use of contraceptives. Additionally, heavy alcohol intake, including binge drinking, can increase the risk of developing medical complications such as blood clots, which may be a concern for some women using hormonal birth control.

Is it Safe to Drink Alcohol on Birth Control?

In general, drinking alcohol while using birth control is safe, but there are some important things to consider. Alcohol leaves the body slower in women on birth control, which may increase the risk of misuse or neglect of contraceptives such as condoms. Drinking too much can also cause women taking birth control pills to forget or miss doses, potentially rendering the birth control ineffective and leading to unplanned pregnancies.

Types of Birth Control and Alcohol's Influence on Effectiveness

Different forms of birth control have varying levels of effectiveness, with abstinence being the only 100% reliable method of preventing pregnancy. For instance, IUDs, implants, injections, and patches are all highly effective forms of birth control, with alcohol use typically not reducing their efficacy. On the other hand, male condoms may be less effective when alcohol is involved, as there's an increased likelihood of misuse or neglect.

Finally, while alcohol does not typically affect the effectiveness of birth control, it's essential to be mindful of its potential impacts on behavior and judgment, as well as the risk of medical complications associated with heavy alcohol intake. Women who have concerns or questions about the use of birth control and alcohol should always consult with their healthcare provider to ensure they're making informed decisions about their health and well-being.

CHAPTER NINE

IS ALCOHOL A CONTROLLED SUBSTANCE?

Why Alcohol Is Regulated, Even Though It's Not a Controlled Substance

While alcohol is not classified as a controlled substance in the United States, its production, distribution, and sale are strictly regulated by the federal government. This is due to the psychoactive properties of alcohol and the potential for dependence and negative health effects associated with its consumption.

Guidelines for alcohol consumption have been established to help prevent harmful use. In the United States alone, there are over 261 alcohol-related deaths each day, with more than 47,000 people per year dying from long-term health issues caused by alcohol consumption. Globally, harmful alcohol use contributes to 3 million deaths each year.

To regulate alcohol, the federal government created the Alcohol and Tobacco Tax and Trade Bureau and the Bureau of Alcohol, Tobacco, Firearms, and Explosives. These agencies oversee the production, distribution, and sale of alcohol to ensure it is handled safely and responsibly.

While alcohol is not a controlled substance like many drugs, it's potential for harm warrants careful regulation and responsible consumption. It's important to be aware of the short-term and long-term effects of alcohol, as well as consumption guidelines, to prevent harmful use.

Consumption Guidelines for Alcohol: How Much Is Too Much?

To help prevent harmful alcohol use, current guidelines recommend limiting alcohol consumption to two drinks or less per day for people of legal drinking age. However, these guidelines vary based on factors such as sex assigned at birth and certain medical conditions.

How Much Is Too Much?

According to the current alcohol consumption guidelines for Americans, cisgender women and others assigned female at birth should consume no more than one drink per day, while cisgender men and others assigned male at birth should consume no more than two drinks per day. It's important to note that the amount of alcohol in a drink can vary, but as a rule, a standard drink contains about 14 grams of pure alcohol.

Who Should Avoid Alcohol?

The guidelines also recommend avoiding alcohol entirely if you are under the minimum legal drinking age in the United States (which is 21), pregnant or think you might be, taking medications known to interact with alcohol, have a medical condition that can be made worse by alcohol, are recovering from alcohol use disorder, or are unable to control how much you drink. It's also important to avoid alcohol if you are planning to drive a vehicle or operate machinery.

In conclusion, understanding these guidelines and being aware of your personal alcohol consumption can help you make informed choices about your drinking habits and reduce your risk of developing alcohol-related health problems.

The Immediate and Potential Lasting Effects of Short-Term Alcohol Use

When you consume alcohol, it can bring on a range of sensations that might be pleasurable, like a relaxed feeling or euphoria. But it can also lead to lowered inhibitions, impulsive behavior, and mood changes that can impact your safety and well-being. Some other effects you might experience include slurred speech, dizziness, and changes in perception. These effects can be temporary, but their consequences can last much longer. Impaired judgment and coordination can increase the risk of accidents, injuries, and violence. So, it's important to be mindful of the potential consequences of short-term alcohol use, no matter how enjoyable it might feel in the moment.

The Long-Term Complications of Excessive Alcohol Use

Long-term or excessive alcohol use can have serious and lasting effects on both your physical and mental health, as well as on those around you.

Here are some of the most common long-term effects:

- **Poor Mental Health:** Long-term alcohol use can lead to depression and anxiety, which can exacerbate existing mental health conditions or even trigger new ones.

- **Impaired Memory or Concentration:** Chronic alcohol use can damage the brain and impair memory and concentration, making it difficult to learn and retain new information.

- **Sexual Dysfunction**: Alcohol use can lead to sexual dysfunction in both men and women, including erectile dysfunction and premature ejaculation.

- **Weakened Immune System:** Drinking excessively weakens your immune system, making you more susceptible to illnesses and infections.
- **Pancreatitis:** Heavy drinking can cause inflammation of the pancreas, a serious and painful condition that can lead to long-term health problems.
- **Liver Disease:** Excessive alcohol use can cause liver damage, leading to liver disease, cirrhosis, and even liver failure.
- **Cardiovascular Disease**: Heavy drinking can increase your risk of high blood pressure, heart disease, and stroke.
- **Cancer:** Excessive alcohol use is linked to an increased risk of several types of cancer, including breast, colon, liver, mouth, throat, oesophageal, and stomach cancer.

It's important to remember that these effects can take years to develop and may not be immediately noticeable. However, by reducing or eliminating your alcohol intake, you can significantly reduce your risk of developing these serious health complications.

Regulating Controlled and Uncontrolled Substances:

Understanding the Difference

The Controlled Substances Act (CSA) is a federal law that regulates drugs and other substances based on their potential for misuse, dependence, and danger to the public. The Act classifies substances into different schedules based on their medical use, risk of abuse, and potential for dependence. Controlled substances with medical use, such as Valium and morphine, are available only by prescription from a licensed medical professional, whereas those without medical use, such as heroin, are illegal in the United States.

On the other hand, uncontrolled substances such as alcohol can be used by anyone, and individual states determine how it is imported, distributed, and sold, as well as who can possess it. However, the production, distribution, and sale of alcohol are federally regulated by the Alcohol and Tobacco Tax and Trade Bureau and the Bureau of Alcohol, Tobacco, Firearms, and Explosives due to its potential health risks.

While the use of controlled substances is highly regulated and restricted to medical purposes, uncontrolled substances like alcohol can have significant consequences when consumed in excess or over a long period of time. Understanding the differences between these two types of substances is crucial to make informed decisions about their use and minimize the associated risks.

CHAPTER TEN

The Stages of Alcoholism: Understanding the Progression of Addiction

Alcoholism is a chronic and progressive disease that can have severe physical, mental, and social consequences. Understanding the stages of alcoholism can help individuals recognize the signs and symptoms of addiction and seek help before it's too late.

The Four Stages of Alcoholism:

1. **Pre-Alcoholic Stage** - characterized by occasional or social drinking that does not lead to dependency or addiction.

2. **Early-Alcoholic Stage** - marked by an increased tolerance to alcohol, frequent drinking, and an increased need for alcohol to function.

3. **Middle-Alcoholic Stage** - marked by a loss of control over alcohol use, blackouts, and impaired social and occupational functioning.

4. **Late-Alcoholic Stage** - characterized by a physical and psychological dependence on alcohol, severe withdrawal symptoms, and the potential for life-threatening consequences.

Signs and Symptoms of Each Stage:

Each stage of alcoholism is associated with specific signs and symptoms that can help individuals and their loved ones recognize a problem and seek help.

Pre-Alcoholic Stage:

- Social or occasional drinking
- Low tolerance to alcohol
- No physical or psychological dependence
- No withdrawal symptoms
- No negative consequences

Early-Alcoholic Stage:

- Increased tolerance to alcohol
- Frequent drinking
- Increased need for alcohol to function.

- Denial of a drinking problem
- Mood swings and irritability
- Minor blackouts and memory lapses
- Difficulty meeting responsibilities

Middle-Alcoholic Stage:

- Loss of control over alcohol use
- Increased blackouts and memory lapses
- Impaired judgment and decision-making
- Risky behaviors (e.g., drinking and driving)
- Legal problems (e.g., DUI)
- Relationship and work problems
- Financial difficulties

Late-Alcoholic Stage:

- Physical and psychological dependence on alcohol
- Severe withdrawal symptoms (e.g., seizures, delirium tremens)
- Inability to stop drinking despite negative consequences.
- Increased tolerance to alcohol

- Serious health consequences (e.g., liver damage, brain damage)
- Potential for death from alcohol-related causes

Treatment Options:

There are various treatment options available for alcoholism, including therapy, medication, and support groups. Early intervention is crucial to preventing the progression of alcoholism and reducing the risk of serious health consequences.

CHAPTER ELEVEN

How to Break Free from Alcohol Addiction without AA: Expert Tips and Strategies

How to Quit Drinking without Alcoholics Anonymous

If you're struggling with alcohol addiction and don't want to attend Alcoholics Anonymous (AA), don't worry. There are several other options available to help you quit drinking. One such option is the CORE process, which stands for Commit, Objectify, Respond, and Enjoy. By using these techniques, you can overcome your addiction quietly and for free in the comfort of your own home.

> ➤ **Understanding Your Drinking Problem**

Before you begin using the CORE process, it's essential to understand why you drink. While Alcoholics Anonymous views alcoholism as a disease that only a Higher Power can cure, other models of alcohol dependence exist outside AA. A useful way to think about a drinking problem is in terms of survival instincts. The brain is divided into two parts: the human brain (you) and the animal brain (it). The animal brain is concerned only with survival and falsely believes that you need alcohol to survive when you're chemically dependent on it. It's what we call the "booze brain." Lacking an understanding of how alcohol impacts the brain can lead one to be easily misled by its influence and give in to drinking.

> ### ➤ Using the CORE Process

The CORE process involves four simple steps. First, commit yourself to permanent abstinence from alcohol. Tell yourself that you don't need alcohol to survive, plan to quit for good, and say the words "I will never drink again." Experiencing emotions such as fear, panic, anger, depression, or physical discomfort does not warrant alarm or undue concern. Your body has been dependent on alcohol for a long time, and it will take some time to adjust.

Second, objectify your booze brain. The human brain is more intelligent than the booze brain, which doesn't understand that you can live without alcohol. Referring to the effects of alcohol as "it" rather than "I" can help to objectify the influence of alcohol on the brain. By doing so, one can recognize that alcohol holds no sway over them, and they retain control over their actions. The booze brain will try anything to get you to drink because it falsely believes that you need alcohol to survive. Any thought or emotion that entices one to drink is a manifestation of the influence of alcohol on the brain, attempting to deceive the individual.

Third, respond to your booze brain by saying "never" whenever you hear it asking for a drink. This will cause the booze brain to back down because it recognizes that it is not in control, and there is no way it can force you to drink. When offered a drink by friends, one can decline by politely saying, "No thanks, I'm quitting." If someone wishes to avoid further discussion on the topic, they can opt to respond with "I'm slowing down" or a straightforward "No, thanks." Finally, enjoy your recovery from alcohol dependence. Remind yourself that by making this choice, you are actively striving to become a happier and healthier individual. Think about alternative drinks you can have when you're spending time with friends, such as mocktails, alcohol-free beer, or soda. By using these techniques and staying committed, you can overcome alcohol addiction without Alcoholics Anonymous.

Alcohol addiction is a tough battle, but it's not one that you must fight alone. While Alcoholics Anonymous (AA) has long been the go-to support group for those seeking sobriety, it's not the only option available. From mindfulness-based recovery communities to self-empowering support groups, there are now endless options to choose from. In this article, *we'll explore some tips and strategies on how to quit drinking without going to AA.*

Find Support in a Different Group

If AA isn't the right fit for you, don't despair. There are many other support groups out there that may be more aligned with your recovery style and beliefs. For example, Yoga of 12-Step Recovery connects yoga techniques with practical tools of 12-step recovery, while Smart Recovery offers a self-empowering approach to addiction recovery. If none of these options appeal to you, you can even start your own group on social networking sites like Facebook.

Talk with a Coach, Therapist, or Counselor

Coaching or therapy can be a valuable tool in your sobriety journey. Many trained professionals, including coaches, counselors, and psychologists, are available to support you on your path to recovery. Seeing a psychiatrist can also be helpful, particularly if you have underlying anxiety or depression that you were self-medicating with alcohol.

Go Online

Online programs are another convenient way to get support in quitting drinking. Workit Health, for example, offers online, science-backed courses to help you beat alcoholism. Whether or not you choose to use 12-step methods is entirely up to you.

Talk to Your Doctor

Medication can also be an effective tool in treating alcoholism. Medications like Antabuse, Naltrexone, Campral, and Topomax are used to treat alcoholism and can be prescribed by your doctor.

Work Out

Exercise can be a game-changer in early sobriety. It not only boosts brain function, but also reduces cravings and improves overall well-being. Incorporating exercise into your daily routine can be a powerful tool in overcoming alcohol addiction.

Change Your Social Scene

Changing your social scene is crucial to breaking free from addiction. AA provides a new social scene filled with people who understand your struggles, but there are other ways to find sober friends. Meetup offers great local activities to meet new people in positive environments.

Get Spiritual

Spirituality is an integral part of many recovery programs, including AA. It helps you find a power greater than yourself and encourages involvement in service to others. Whether or not you choose to follow a spiritual program, finding a purpose in life beyond alcohol can be a great motivator in your recovery journey.

Finally, there are many ways to quit drinking without AA. Recovery is a personal journey, and no two paths will look the same. Whether you choose to join a different support group, talk to a therapist, or incorporate exercise into your routine, the most important thing is to find a method that works for you. With the right tools and support, you can break free from alcohol addiction and create a fulfilling life in sobriety.

CHAPTER TWELVE

Life After Recovery: Navigating Relationships, Careers, and Finding Purpose

Congratulations, you have taken the brave step towards recovery from alcohol addiction! Recovery is a journey, not a destination. And while it may feel like the hardest part is behind you, the road ahead may be equally challenging. Life after recovery can be a daunting prospect, but it can also be an exciting and rewarding one.

Achieving sobriety is a significant accomplishment, but the journey to recovery doesn't end there. Individuals in recovery often face challenges in navigating relationships, and careers and finding meaning and purpose in their lives. This chapter will provide guidance on how to build a fulfilling life after recovery.

Rebuilding Relationships:

One of the most challenging aspects of life after recovery can be rebuilding relationships with those who were affected by your addiction. Relationships with family, friends, and loved ones can be strained due to past behaviors, and it can take time and effort to repair them. Communication is key in rebuilding relationships. It is important to be honest with those you have hurt, apologize for your past behavior, and make amends. It is also important to set boundaries and communicate your needs, while also respecting the needs and boundaries of others.

Addiction can take a toll on relationships with family, friends, and partners. Rebuilding trust and repairing relationships can be challenging, but it's an essential part of the recovery process. This chapter will explore strategies for repairing relationships, setting boundaries, and developing healthy communication skills.

- Acknowledge the harm done to loved ones.
- Apologize and make amends.
- Set healthy boundaries.
- Develop healthy communication skills.
- Attend family therapy.

Building a Career:

Recovery can also present opportunities for growth in your career. Many people who struggle with addiction experience setbacks in their professional lives, but with recovery, you can rebuild your career with newfound determination and focus. If you are currently employed, it may be helpful to speak with your employer about your recovery and any support you may need. If you are seeking new employment, consider looking for work that aligns with your values and purpose. Many people in recovery find that volunteering or pursuing a new career path brings them fulfillment and purpose. Many individuals in recovery face challenges in building or maintaining a career.

Strategies for finding employment, managing workplace triggers, and developing healthy coping mechanisms.

- Build a supportive network.
- Be honest about past struggles.
- Explore new career paths.
- Develop healthy coping mechanisms.
- Manage stress and anxiety.
- Seek professional help if necessary.

Finding Purpose:

One of the most significant benefits of recovery is the opportunity to rediscover your sense of purpose. For many people, addiction can be a way of numbing difficult emotions or coping with past traumas. In recovery, you can begin to work through these emotions and heal from past wounds, allowing you to find your true purpose in life. This may involve exploring new interests or hobbies, setting new goals, or pursuing a long-held dream.

Life after recovery can be a time of great transformation, but it can also be challenging. Remember to take it one day at a time and be gentle with yourself. Recovery is a journey, and it takes time and effort to build a fulfilling and purposeful life. With the right mindset, tools, and support, you can navigate the challenges of life after recovery and build a life you love.

CONCLUSION

Congratulations on completing Mind Over Matter: How to Harness Your Thoughts to Conquer Alcohol and Create a Life You Love. I hope that this book has provided you with the knowledge, tools, and strategies to overcome alcohol addiction, understand the science behind alcohol, and explore its effects on different aspects of life.

From understanding the science behind alcohol to breaking free from addiction, this book has provided an in-depth analysis of alcohol addiction, its stages, triggers, and effects on mental and physical health. It has also provided readers with essential information on drinking with diabetes, the intersection of birth control and alcohol, and the effects of alcohol on cholesterol levels and blood pressure.

Most importantly, Chapter Twelve offers invaluable insights into life after recovery, providing a roadmap to individuals who have overcome alcohol addiction and are ready to take on the next chapter of their lives. I hope that this book has empowered you to take control of your life and make positive changes that will help you create a life you love.

Dear Readers,

Thank you for joining me on this journey to explore the complex relationship between alcohol and our bodies, minds, and lives. I hope you found this book informative, thought-provoking, and empowering.

As we come to the end of this book, I want to take a moment to express my deep gratitude to every one of you for your time, attention, and engagement. Writing this book has been a labor of love and knowing that it may make a positive difference in someone's life is a tremendous source of joy and fulfillment.

If you enjoyed this book and found it helpful, I would be immensely grateful if you could take a few moments to leave a short review on the bookstore page. Your feedback and support mean the world to me, and I will always be happy to reply to your review or answer any questions you may have.

Thank you again for your trust and support. I wish you all the best on your journey to health, happiness, and purpose.

Warmly,

DARYL TYLER.

Printed in Great Britain
by Amazon

46884306R00056